UNDERSTANDING PARANORMAL

INVESTIGATING ZOMBIES AND THE LIVING DEAD

MARY-LANE KAMBERG

Britannica
Educational Publishing

IN ASSOCIATION WITH

ROSEN
EDUCATIONAL SERVICES

For Ronin Rohrback

Published in 2015 by Britannica Educational Publishing (a trademark of Encyclopædia Britannica, Inc.) in association with The Rosen Publishing Group, Inc.
29 East 21st Street, New York, NY 10010

Copyright © 2015 The Rosen Publishing Group, Inc., and Encyclopædia Britannica, Inc. Encyclopædia Britannica, Britannica, and the Thistle logo are registered trademarks of Encyclopædia Britannica, Inc. All rights reserved.

Distributed exclusively by Rosen Publishing.
To see additional Britannica Educational Publishing titles, go to rosenpublishing.com.

First Edition

Britannica Educational Publishing
J. E. Luebering: Director, Core Reference Group
Anthony L. Green: Editor, Compton's by Britannica

Rosen Publishing
Hope Lourie Killcoyne: Executive Editor
Jacob R. Steinberg: Editor
Nelson Sá: Art Director
Michael Moy: Designer
Cindy Reiman: Photography Manager
Karen Huang: Photo Research

Cataloging-in-Publication Data

Kamberg, Mary-Lane, 1948–
Investigating zombies and the living dead/Mary-Lane Kamberg.—First Edition.
     pages cm.—(Understanding the paranormal)
Includes bibliographical references and index.
ISBN 978-1-62275-871-5 (library bound)—ISBN 978-1-62275-872-2 (pbk.)—
ISBN 978-1-62275-875-3 (6-pack)
1. Zombies. I. Title.
GR581.K36 2014
398.21—dc23

2014026107

Manufactured in the United States of America

Photo credits: Cover, p. 1 Linda Bucklin/Shutterstock.com; p. 5 © AMC/Courtesy Everett Collection; p 7 © Entertainment Pictures/ZUMA Press; p. 9 Dieter Spears/E+/Getty Images; p. 11 © Photos.com/Thinkstock; pp. 13, 19 Thony Belizaire/AFP/Getty Images; p. 14 BSIP/Universal Images Group/Getty Images; p. 16 Iberfoto/SuperStock; p. 18 Forum/Hulton Fine Art/Getty Images; p. 21 © Entertainment Pictures/ZUMA Press; p. 22 Archive Photos/Moviepix/Getty Images; p. 25 De Agostini/Getty Images; p. 26 Fotosearch/Archive Photos/Getty Images; pp. 28-29 Jean-Claude Francolon/Gamma-Rapho/Getty Images; p. 30 Rick Madonik/Toronto Star/Getty Images; p. 31 Beth Swanson/Shutterstock.com; p. 34 © MCA/Universal/Courtesy: Everett Collection; p. 35 Carley Margolis/FilmMagic/Getty Images; p. 37 Nemar74/Shutterstock.com; p. 39 CDC; p. 41 © AP Images; interior pages background images © iStockphoto.com/Kivilvim Pinar, © iStockphoto.com/mitja2.

CONTENTS

INTRODUCTION

In Haitian folklore, they once lived as humans, died, and were buried. They were then brought forth from the grave to serve as slaves. Through powerful forces of witchcraft, their bodies remained preserved, carrying out the bidding of the sorcerer at whose hands they had been revived. They shuffled along, mindlessly working the sugarcane plantations of Haiti. They were zombies.

Later, Western popular culture turned zombies into superhuman, undead creatures. These walking dead raced through cities and the countryside in search of human brains to eat. While the zombie of Haitian folklore is subordinate to a master, these later, horror-film–fueled varieties obey only an overwhelming desire for human flesh. As they attack their victims, they create more of their kind—the living dead.

Zombies have become a frequent feature in works of horror fiction and film. In fact, the zombies of contemporary film were largely the innovation of American filmmaker George A. Romero. But the idea of the zombie has its roots in the folklore of Haiti. In the pages to come, we will explore the transformation of this fascinating figure from Haitian tradition into one of contemporary pop culture's favorite creatures.

Novelists and filmmakers built on the idea of the zombie in books, movies, and television shows, as in this scene from the AMC network's The Walking Dead.

CHAPTER ONE

THE WORLD OF THE LIVING DEAD

I n a story about zombies, a man was believed to be dead, and so he was buried. Owing to witchcraft, radiation, or infection, however, his body was able to rise back up and leave the grave. He is not exactly dead, but he is not truly alive, either. He has joined the ranks of the "undead." The man has become a zombie.

Zombies are fictional monsters featured in books, films, and video games. Their traits differ according to where they appear, but they all have their roots in Haitian folklore. According to Haitian legend, zombies are slaves with no minds of their own. Unlike their movie counterparts, however, the classic zombies of Haitian lore are typically not dangerous.

Zombies vary from wandering beings who shuffle their feet to bloodthirsty monsters with superhuman speed on the hunt for human brains to eat.

WHAT ARE ZOMBIES LIKE?

Authors, video game designers, and Hollywood moviemakers have added more and more elements to zombie behavior. In doing so, they've also invented much of the danger that zombies are said to pose. The word "zombie" has been used for beings with varying characteristics, but they all share a few of the same traits.

Most important is a lack of free will. Zombies blindly obey either their masters or their own strong desire for such things as revenge, violence, or human flesh. In Haitian folklore, they perform manual labor and work the fields or even serve as bookkeepers or shop workers. In horror films and video games, they violently attack humans, typically lunging at defenseless victims to eat their brains. The sole purpose of zombies is to get whatever they—or their masters—desire.

Any human can become a zombie, and in some stories, there are even zombie animals. (The 2006 New Zealand comedy-horror film *Black Sheep* features a flock of zombie sheep.) Some tales tell of magic spells that take the spirit of a human and revive it in a cow or a pig to be sold at the marketplace.

In addition to missing a life force, some pop culture representations of zombies are missing arms or legs, too. These limbs may have been used in sacrifices or in the making of magic potions. Oftentimes, their bodies are depicted as being covered in blood or with open wounds. While the zombies of Haitian tradition are said to be well preserved through magic, Hollywood zombies often have rotting bodies and give off a sickening smell.

The zombies of pop culture are strong. Despite this strength, they have trouble getting around. When they walk, they typically shuffle their feet in a slow, lazy movement called shambling. Only recently have movies and video games sometimes given them superhuman speed to match their strength.

Hollywood and pop culture have reimagined zombies as rotting creatures that are often missing limbs or large portions of skin. Furthermore they are depicted as aggressive creatures hungry for human flesh.

THE BIRTH OF THE UNDEAD

Early stories about zombies were told in Haiti, where African slaves practiced a religion called Vodou. Vodou is related to what is called Voodoo in the United

WHAT'S IN A NAME?

No one knows with certainty the exact roots of the word "zombie," but scholars have come up with several ideas. The word "zombi," spelled without the "e," is said to have first appeared printed in English in Robert Southey's book *History of Brazil,* published in 1810–19. Southey's "Zombi" was a West African term for a deity, or god—nothing like the zombies of today's horror films.

Some possible linguistic sources of the word "zombie" include:

- *nzambi* "God" or "spirit of a dead person" in Kongo and Kimbundu, languages spoken in Central Africa.
- *zumbi* "Fetish" (an object believed to have supernatural or magical powers) in Kongo.
- *jumbie* "Evil spirit" or "ghost" in several Caribbean countries.

States and Vodun in West Africa. Vodou is a religion that developed out of the spiritual beliefs of people of various African ethnic groups who were enslaved and brought to colonial Haiti. It also incorporated elements of Roman Catholicism spread by missionaries in the 16th and 17th centuries. The word "Vodou" means "spirit" or "deity" in the Fon language of Benin.

According to Haitian folklore, priest-like magicians called *bokor* use witchcraft to create zombies to serve as slaves. Some researchers believe *bokor* may

West Africans captured by slave traders brought their Vodun religion with them on the voyage across the Atlantic Ocean to colonial Haiti.

target people to become zombies as punishment for social misconduct.

As is often the case with folklore, there are many different stories of how to create a zombie. There are primarily two types of zombies: a soul without a body, or a *zombi astral*, and a body without a soul, or a *zombi corps cadavre*. Generally, a *bokor* who wants to make a zombie begins while the person is still alive. The *bokor* removes a part of the person's soul. Losing this part of the soul eventually causes the person to die. When the victim dies, he or she is buried. (In other tales, the soul remains with the deceased for a few days after death, and the *bokor* can steal the soul after the person has died.)

While the soul without a body is, in fact, more common in Haitian folklore, it is not the zombie with which most readers are familiar. To create a body without a soul (the type of zombie that made it big in Hollywood), the *bokor* has to use the stolen part of a person's soul for further magic, including reviving the person's corpse.

The *bokor* visits the graveyard and sneaks up to the person's grave. A spirit called Baron Samedi, "the protector of the dead," guards the cemetery. The protector won't let the body be removed unless the *bokor* tricks him to sleep with a magic spell.

Once the protector falls asleep, the *bokor* stands in front of the headstone. Through spells and rituals, the *bokor* is said to be able to make the body come to "life."

Modern Haitians honor the "grave" of the Vodun spirit Baron Samedi as part of the Roman Catholic celebrations of All Saints' Day and All Souls' Day.

GETTING RID OF ZOMBIES

In movies, books, and games, doing away with the undead proves to be no easy task. According to most legends, zombies cannot simply be killed because they are already

OTHER WAYS TO MAKE A ZOMBIE

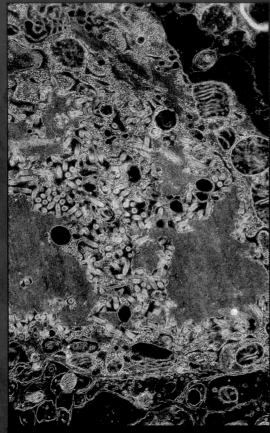

In some films, infection with a virus— such as the rabies virus shown here— turns healthy humans into zombies. These monsters in turn infect more humans to create more zombies.

Books, movies, and video games have come up with new, creative ways to make zombies. In some stories, radiation exposure turns living humans into zombielike monsters or revives the dead. Alternatively, zombies themselves may turn living humans into new zombies by biting or killing them.

Viruses and poisons are also to blame. In the *Resident Evil* video games and movies, either parasites, viruses, or neurotoxins (poisons that act on the nervous system) turn victims into zombies. In the movie *28 Days Later* (2002), a virus is responsible for creating the monsters.

dead. Fire and bright lights often scare zombies away, but nothing seems to injure them. In classic horror films, trying to stop them with traditional weapons won't work. If someone shoots or stabs them, they feel no pain. They just keep shambling forward. Most movie protagonists must find an innovative way to destroy a zombie's brain.

In traditional Haitian lore, a zombie is said to be able to regain his senses by eating salt. A smart master keeps his zombies away from salt—for fear that the zombies may rebel and kill him. In other variations of the folklore, a freed zombie might simply return to the grave and rest in peace.

CHAPTER TWO

FROM AFRICA TO THE BIG SCREEN

S tories of the walking dead have existed in different cultures in Africa and the Caribbean for hundreds of years. Zombie legends were not widely known in the Western world, however, until the early twentieth century, when a U.S. author described them in a popular travel book. The idea of the zombie soon captured the imaginations of many people in the United States, and the zombie began to star in Hollywood films.

Western visitors to Haiti were largely responsible for bringing zombie folklore back to the United States, where it was previously little known.

AFRICAN ROOTS

Haitian zombie legends may stem from African folklore about the living dead. In several African cultures, including in Benin, Tanzania, and South Africa, sorcerers are said to be able to rouse the dead and enslave them. In two cultures in Central Africa, magical powders are thought to be used. As in Haiti, zombies in Africa include souls without a body as well as bodies without a soul.

Haitian folklore about zombies is informed by beliefs about human souls and the spirit world in the Haitian religion Vodou. Vodou has its roots in the traditional West African religion Vodun. The Vodun religion shares many elements with other world religions. Followers believe in one creator God. They also believe in many other gods and spirits that rule the human world. Vodun believers think that gods can inhabit human bodies and speak through them. According to Vodun, humans become spirits after death.

Beginning about the early 1500s, slave traders kidnapped countless Africans and sold them in the Americas. These slaves brought their religion and folklore with them to the New World. Living in the Americas, many African slaves continued their practices of Vodun. Fearful of slave revolts, white slave owners saw Vodun rituals as acts of evil witchcraft. Slave owners outlawed the religion.

A centuries-old Roman Catholic painting from Poland known as the **Black Madonna of Czestochowa** *has served as the basis for Haitian images that blend Catholic and Vodun traditions.*

In an attempt to replace Vodun, Roman Catholic priests taught the slaves about Christianity. Some aspects of the Catholic faith were seen as similar to concepts in Vodun. For example, both Catholicism and Vodun teach that multiple spirits—saints in Catholicism and *lwa* in Vodun—were once humans. After death, these spirits take on special duties for the living.

Despite the ban on Vodun, slaves still practiced it in secret. They disguised their beliefs, mixing Vodun observances with certain Catholic rituals. Other beliefs and rituals from the native Indians called Taino, or Arawak, were mixed in as

Practitioners of Vodou pray to the spirit of motherhood, romance, art, and jealousy as part of a December ceremony that celebrates Christmas.

well. This blend of Vodun, Catholicism, and indigenous beliefs evolved over time into the religion now known as Vodou, or Voodoo.

Today, an estimated sixty million people follow Vodun, Vodou, or Voodoo. They live primarily in the African countries of Benin, Togo, and Ghana, as well as the Caribbean nations of Haiti and the Dominican Republic. Some live in the United States.

TRAVELERS' TALES

In 1884, British diplomat Sir Spenser St. John published a memoir called *Hayti; or, The Black Republic.* In it he described purported Vodou rituals in gory detail. St. John claimed that Haitian Vodou practitioners would cut off human arms and legs to use for sacrifices. He also reported cases of grave robbing and cannibalism. St. John never saw any of these activities for himself; he relied on island gossip to write his stories. His outlandish tales of human sacrifice and cannibalism are today recognized as being inaccurate and indeed racist. Nevertheless, St. John's book spread enduring negative stereotypes about Vodou and Haiti.

In 1929, another nonfiction travel book about Haiti appeared. It was called *The Magic Island*, by William Buehler Seabrook. Seabrook was the first to bring tales of the "Vodou zombi" to wide notice in the world outside Haiti. However, Seabrook never saw any zombies himself. He merely quoted the accounts of others who said that they had witnessed real zombies.

Bela Lugosi stars as "Murder" Legendre, a sorcerer who creates a horde of Haitian zombie slaves in the 1932 film White Zombie.

With sensational accounts such as these, the U.S. entertainment industry took over. Seabrook's book inspired a stage play, *Zombie*, and the first feature-length zombie film, *White Zombie*, both set in Haiti and released in 1932. In the movie, a lovesick man conspires with a sorcerer, played by horror actor Bela Lugosi, to turn a woman into a zombie so that he may control her. The woman dies. After the funeral, the sorcerer uses witchcraft to raise her from the grave. A loose sequel called *Revolt of the Zombies* was released in 1936.

Zombies continued to make it to the big screen in the 1940s with films such as *King of the Zombies* and *I Walked with a Zombie*. With the onset of the atomic age, zombie movies started to include space aliens and radiation. In *Plan 9 from Outer Space* (1959) and *Invisible Invaders* (1959), aliens use zombies to carry out their bidding on Earth.

The biggest development in zombie lore to come out of Hollywood was at the hands of American filmmaker George A. Romero. The 1968 film *Night of the Living Dead* shows humans being attacked by the walking dead. These creatures were a result of exposure to radiation. At the time, Romero called his monsters "ghouls" and "flesh-eaters," not zombies. Nonetheless, popular imagination rebranded the creatures. Most

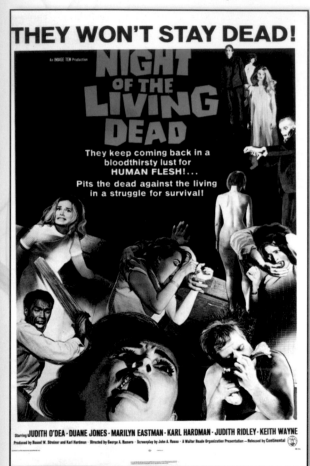

Although George A. Romero's 1968 classic Night of the Living Dead *failed to mention the word "zombie," the film and other movies that followed further defined zombies for moviegoers.*

ZOMBIES AND MINDLESS SHOPPERS?

Owing to American filmmaker George A. Romero's *Night of the Living Dead* (1968), the image of the zombie as a shambling corpse that fed upon the living became a mainstay in film and fiction. Romero intended the film to be more of a social commentary than a monster movie, however. The story centers on the inability of the living to cooperate to save themselves from the threat of undead ghouls.

Romero later revisited his ghouls—now known as zombies, thanks to fans—in a number of related films that feature social or political criticism. He humorously addressed the ills of consumerism—the preoccupation with buying consumer goods—in the gory *Dawn of the Dead* (1978). In that film, a handful of living people attempt to escape the undead by hiding in a shopping mall—and also begin amassing desirable goods. Romero's subsequent zombie movies include *Day of the Dead* (1985), *Land of the Dead* (2005), *Diary of the Dead* (2007), and *Survival of the Dead* (2009).

zombie movies that followed worked with the traits of Romero's monsters. After 1968, zombies craved human flesh and attacked victims with plenty of gore.

CHAPTER THREE

THE ZOMBIE CASEBOOK

On the morning of October 24, 1936, mass hysteria swept through the remote village of Ennery, in north-central Haiti. A barefoot woman limped through town. She looked about 60 years old. Her wrinkled skin was pale. Her eyes were diseased. The sun's glare forced her to cover her face. The woman stood five feet, two inches tall. She weighed less than 100 pounds.

She stopped at one of the nearby farms and told the villagers, "I used to live here." The crowd that gathered included the farm's owner, who recognized the woman as his sister, Felicia Felix-Mentor. Felicia's husband agreed. This woman was his wife. The only problem was that Felicia Felix-Mentor had died and been buried in 1907. The villagers thought she was a zombie.

A third-generation Vodou priest, Hector Hyppolite (1894-1948) of Haiti was also a renowned and prolific painter, primarily of Vodou scenes and symbolism. Shown here is his undated painting The Zombies, *which depicts two bound and restrained zombies who have been removed from their graves and revived by the potion held in the hand of the man wearing a hat and holding the rope.*

This story may sound like the plot of a new movie. However, it's true.

BUT WAS SHE A ZOMBIE?

Haitians widely believed that the dead sometimes came back to life. Family members had little doubt

American author Zora Neale Hurston brought the story of Felicia Felix-Mentor to a U.S. audience in her 1938 anthropological book Tell My Horse. *The author had studied Haitian and Jamaican folklore, including belief in zombies.*

that their relative had returned. The woman looked like Felicia Felix-Mentor. She appeared to be the right age. Her limp seemed to prove it. Family members said that their relative had broken her leg in life and limped as a result.

At a nearby hospital, a doctor named Louis P. Mars x-rayed both of the woman's legs. Neither had ever been broken. The doctor thought her limp resulted from weak muscles caused by a bad diet. With proper nutrition, the woman lost her limp, and she also began to look younger. He diagnosed her with a mental illness called schizophrenia. In other words, he concluded that this was a case of mistaken identity—the woman was not actually Felicia

EXAMINING FELICIA FELIX-MENTOR

In 1945, Louis P. Mars, the doctor who examined the woman thought to be Felicia Felix-Mentor, published an account of his findings in the journal *Man: A Monthly Record of Anthropological Science*. He found that the woman could not give him her name, age, or place of birth. In fact, her answers to the doctor's questions made no sense. Sometimes she burst out in laughter for no reason but showed no emotion at all. She also seemed confused and had lost all sense of time. Based on this examination, Dr. Mars diagnosed her as being schizophrenic, not a zombie.

Felix-Mentor, and she had never died. Mars wrote, the case "gives us an idea of how cases of similar nature are likely to arouse mass hysteria."

BURIED ALIVE

Clairvius Narcisse had a fever. He was gasping for air and coughing up blood. He checked into the Albert Schweitzer Hospital in Deschapelles, Haiti, on April 30, 1962. On May 2, he died. He was buried the next day.

Eighteen years later, Angelina Narcisse, Clairvius's sister, was walking through the village market near her home. A man stopped her and said he was her brother. He used a childhood nickname that only close family members knew. He told her that he had never really died. This is another true story.

Clairvius Narcisse may have been poisoned with "zombie powder." He said that, as the doctors pronounced him dead, he could not move or speak, but he was aware of the doctors pulling a sheet over him. He heard Angelina cry. During the burial, he knew he was being nailed shut in a coffin.

Hours later, a *bokor* dug him up. The *bokor* beat him up, then tied and gagged him. He ended up on a sugar plantation. Narcisse worked there for two years along with other "zombie" slaves until one of them killed the *bokor*. All of the slaves escaped.

Narcisse wandered the countryside, unable to contact his family. He feared that his brother might have

Clairvius Narcisse's family thought that he was long dead. In reality he is thought to have been poisoned and buried alive in a bokor's plot, only to later be resuscitated and used as a "zombie" slave.

hired the *bokor*. The brothers had argued over a piece of property shortly before Narcisse took ill.

Narcisse's story was repeated throughout Haiti. For many, the reports proved what they already believed—that zombies do exist.

THE ZOMBIE PROJECT

Two researchers named Lamarque Douyon and Nathan Kline looked into Clairvius Narcisse's experience. They asked him about family matters about which no stranger could know. His answers fit the facts. Furthermore, the man showed no signs of mental illness or other medical problems, as had been the case with the woman thought to be Felicia Felix-Mentor.

Many Haitians believed that *bokor* used magic to create zombies. Douyon and Kline hypothesized that the *bokor* instead used an unknown drug to paralyze—but

Harvard University anthropologist Wade Davis studied the reports of zombies in Haiti and proposed that victims were poisoned with zombie powder. Other scientists raised doubts about his work.

RECIPE FOR ZOMBIE POWDER

Real-life *bokor* have used "zombie powder" in rituals in Haiti. In the early 1980s, Wade Davis purchased several samples of zombie powder from *bokor* in different parts of Haiti and had the powder scientifically examined. Various samples were found to contain mixtures of the following plants and animals:

- **puffer fish** These fish produce tetrodotoxin, a powerful poison that causes paralysis (loss of muscle function) and sometimes death.
- **cane toads** This species of toad excretes bufotenin, a poison that causes hallucinations.
- *Hyla* **tree frogs** Some species of this genus of tree frogs release irritating substances.

Other ingredients found in the samples included ground-up human remains, glass shards, lizards, worms, and spiders. The analysis of the samples was highly controversial, however. For one thing, some scientists found that tetrodotoxin—thought to be the most important ingredient—was not present or was present in amounts too small to have the intended effect.

The tetrodotoxin produced by puffer fish is more than 1,200 times more poisonous than cyanide. Their name derives from the fact that these fish "puff up" to scare away predators. Some believe the poison they produce is a key ingredient in mixtures known as "zombie powder."

31

not kill—Narcisse. Wade Davis, an anthropologist from Harvard University, joined the scientists in a two-year study called the Zombie Project in 1982–84.

Davis traveled throughout Haiti. He talked to *bokor* and collected samples of "zombie powder." Davis's theory was that poison in zombie powder makes victims appear dead. The *bokor* then dig up the bodies after burial. When the victims come to, they believe they have been turned into zombies. To keep them under control, they are reportedly fed a paste made from a poisonous plant to make them confused and give them hallucinations.

SCIENTISTS SCOFF

Many scientists question Wade Davis's work. Fellow Harvard anthropologist Irven DeVore describes Davis's theory as "interesting but unproven" in an article called "Voodoo Science" published in the April 15, 1988, issue of the journal *Science*.

For instance, Davis reported an experiment that used zombie powder to put animals into a coma-like state. However, he omitted another one in which zombie powder had no effect at all. Those who have studied other reported cases of "real" zombies have decided that they were caused by mental illness or by cases of mistaken identity. So far, no one has scientifically proven that drugs are being used to make "zombies."

CHAPTER FOUR

THE DEAD RISE AGAIN

As anthropologists worked to understand the purported cases of zombies roaming Haitian fields, another field entirely found itself slowly taken over by zombies—popular culture. In recent years, zombies have become such a huge part of pop culture that even the U.S. Centers for Disease Control and Prevention has jokingly issued zombie survival kits and preparedness guides. Zombies now appear in movies, books, and just about all forms of entertainment.

THE ZOMBIE RESURGENCE

Romero's *Night of the Living Dead* helped give zombies a major boost into the public spotlight. Since the 1980s,

Dancing zombies invaded the music video world in singer Michael Jackson's 1983 hit "Thriller."

the zombie invasion has spread from horror flicks to other genres of movies and to television, books, and other media. Singer Michael Jackson, for example, featured a troupe of dancing zombies in his 1983 hit music video "Thriller."

At the movies, the horror films of the 1930s–60s gave way to zombie comedy with such films as 1984's *Night of the Comet*, in which a couple of teenagers survive an encounter with a massive comet that turns most of the human race into zombies. Another standout zombie flick of the 1980s was *The Return of the Living Dead* (1985), in which a group of teenage punks must fight off bands of brain-eating zombies.

With the turn of the millennium, the zombie subgenre experienced its biggest surge yet. American horror author Max Brooks published *The Zombie Survival Guide* in 2003 and the top-selling novel *World War Z: An Oral History of the Zombie War* in 2006. *World War Z* was made into a film in 2013. Horror writer Stephen King published

Zombie toys, games, and costumes are now rather widespread. Filmmaker George A. Romero, who made the classic Night of the Living Dead, *poses with a plastic zombie doll.*

an apocalyptic zombie novel titled *Cell* in 2006. The comic-book series *The Walking Dead*, which began in 2003, was converted into a highly popular TV series in 2010.

The 2009 release of Seth Grahame-Smith's *Pride and Prejudice and Zombies* ushered in a new genre of literary monster mashups. A literary mashup is a humorous tale that combines a pre-existing work of literature with elements from a different genre—in this case, horror fiction. Grahame-Smith's novel added zombies to the classic tale of *Pride and Prejudice* by Jane Austen.

In the mashup, Austen's heroine, Elizabeth Bennet, and her four sisters learn to use weapons and martial arts to protect themselves from zombies near their home. The success of the book encouraged author Steve Hockensmith to write two more *Pride and Prejudice* zombie mashups: *Dawn of the Dreadfuls* (2010) and *Dreadfully Ever After (2011)*.

THE ZOMBIE APOCALYPSE

A popular concept that developed with the revival of the zombie genre was that of the zombie apocalypse. The idea of the zombie apocalypse presents the end of the world or widespread destruction at the hands of zombies. In works depicting zombie apocalypses, either a plague or radiation causes zombies to outnumber humans. Those who remain must battle for survival.

While it is unlikely that humanity will soon be fighting off flesh-hungry creatures, the zombie take-over of pop culture has been evident. Zombies have even "come to life" off the big screen. Since the early 2000s, mobs of people have dressed up in zombie costumes and taken "zombie walks" in cities around the world. Instructors in zombie-themed fitness classes teach participants how to survive a zombie apocalypse—and simultaneously how to get a good workout.

The zombie revival has achieved global interest. In October 2013, a "zombie mob" paraded in Belgrade, Serbia, to promote a Serbian science-fiction movie festival.

Several U.S. colleges and universities, from California to Florida and New York, have had zombie clubs. Depending on the club, members have promoted "zombie awareness," folklore appreciation, or preparation for a zombie apocalypse or have planned zombie-related activities and community service.

ZOMBIE PREPAREDNESS

Even the U.S. Centers for Disease Control and Prevention has given in to the zombie craze. In 2011, it began to promote zombie preparedness with a tongue-in-cheek graphic novel and article on its public health blog. The true purpose of the campaign was to promote preparedness tips for real disasters.

On the CDC website, Dr. Ali Khan, director of the Office of Public Health Preparedness and Response, wrote, "If you are generally well equipped to deal with a zombie apocalypse, you will be prepared for a hurricane, pandemic, earthquake, or terrorist attack." All you need is an emergency kit and a plan. The kit should contain basic emergency items. The plan should identify a place to meet family members, a contact list that includes "your local zombie response team," and evacuation routes.

The Centers for Disease Control and Prevention jumped on the zombie bandwagon, with recommendations for a survival kit for a zombie apocalypse—as well as other disasters.

The evacuation routes are most important. According to the CDC, "When zombies are hungry they won't stop until they get food . . . you need to get out of town fast! Plan where you would go and multiple routes you would take ahead of time so that the flesh eaters don't have a chance! This is also helpful when natural disasters strike and you have to take shelter fast."

ZOMBIE ATTACK SURVIVAL KIT

According to a humorous campaign of the Centers for Disease Control and Prevention, in the event of a zombie apocalypse, a zombie survival kit "will get you through the first couple of days before you can locate a zombie-free refugee camp." The kit can also be used for real emergencies. The essential components of a zombie survival kit include:

- Water (one gallon per person per day)
- Food that won't spoil
- Medicine
- Tools
- Soap and towels
- A blanket and a change of clothes for each family member
- Important documents (such as birth certificates, passports, etc.)
- First-aid supplies

TOYS AND GAMES

The zombie invasion took video games in 1996. That's the year that the first game in the *Resident Evil* series came out, and it was followed by several sequels for various game consoles. *Resident Evil* has been one of modern gaming's most popular and critically acclaimed series. The franchise features video games, toys, films, novels, and comic books.

The House of the Dead, a light-gun arcade game, was released in 1997. It spawned several sequels and a 2003 film. Other zombie-themed video games such as *Dead*

In the survival horror video game Resident Evil 6 *from Japanese company Capcom, characters fight the force behind a massive bio-terrorist attack. The game is marketed worldwide.*

Rising (2006) and *Left 4 Dead (2008)* were also followed by popular sequels. Zombies even found their way into popular board games. In games such as Zombicide and Zombie Kidz, players must use teamwork to fight against the undead. It goes without saying that no toy chest is complete without zombie action figures.

CONCLUSION

Over a wide variety of media, the zombie image has changed over time. The slow-moving, enslaved creature of Haitian lore has become a superhuman, raging monster that moviegoers, readers, and fans of horror can't get enough of. From West African rituals and zombie sightings in Haiti, the world of the undead has grown to include profitable Western tourist, entertainment, and toy industries. Whether traditional, sluggish monsters or their countless modern variations, good luck trying to fight off the zombie invasion.

GLOSSARY

ANTHROPOLOGIST A social scientist who studies humans' physical and cultural development.

BOKOR A priest-like magician who performs rituals and is believed to have the power to create zombies.

BUFOTENIN Produced by the cane toad, a poison that causes hallucinations.

CANNIBALISM The eating of human flesh by a human being, sometimes as part of a religious practice.

COMA A state of deep unconsciousness, in which the brain functions only at the lowest level and the patient fails to respond to sounds or activity.

CORPSE A dead body, usually referring to that of a human being.

EVACUATION The act of leaving a dangerous place as a protective measure.

GORE Blood that has been shed from an injury, especially as a result of fighting, murder, or other violence.

HALLUCINATION An experience of something, such as a sight, sound, or smell, that does not really exist.

PANDEMIC An outbreak of disease that affects large numbers of people throughout a widespread area, such as an entire country, a continent, or even the whole world.

PARALYZE To make a person or part of the body unable to move.

SCHIZOPHRENIA A serious mental illness that is characterized by a distorted understanding of the world, by greatly reduced ability to carry out one's daily tasks, and by abnormal ways of thinking, feeling, and behaving.

TETRODOTOXIN A poison produced by puffer fish that can cause paralysis and sometimes death in humans.

VODOU A religion found predominantly in Haiti. It is related to American Voodoo and West African Vodun.

ZOMBI ASTRAL A type of zombie that is a soul without a body, often sold in bottles or used in ceremonies.

ZOMBI CORPS CADAVRE A type of zombie that is a body without a soul, dug from its grave and revived after death.

ZOMBIE APOCALYPSE In films, games, and novels, the end of the world or widespread destruction at the hands of zombies.

FOR FURTHER READING

Anderson, M.T. *Zombie Mommy*. New York, NY: Beach Lane Books, 2012.

Holbrook, Sara. *Zombies! Evacuate the School!* Honesdale, PA: Wordsong, 2010.

Hutton, Clare. *Zombie Dog*. New York, NY: Scholastic Rotten Apple, 2012.

Inguanzo, Ozzy. *Zombies on Film: The Definitive Story of Undead Cinema*. New York, NY: Rizzoli, 2014.

Johnson, Rebecca L. *Zombie Makers: True Stories of Nature's Undead*. Minneapolis, MN: 21st Century, 2012.

Kay, Glenn. *Zombie Movies: The Ultimate Guide*. Chicago, IL: Chicago Review Press, 2012.

Kloepfer, John, and Steve Wolfhard. *The Zombie Chasers*. New York, NY: HarperCollins, 2010.

Luber, David. *Enter the Zombie*. New York, NY: Starscape, 2011.

McMurtry, Ken. *Zombie Penpal*. Waitsfield, VT: Choose Your Own Adventure, 2011.

Mogk, Matt. *Everything You Ever Wanted to Know About Zombies*. New York, NY: Gallery Books, 2011.

Moskowitz, Hannah. *Zombie Tag*. New York, NY: Roaring Book Press, 2011.

Stine, R.L. *Goosebumps Hall of Horrors #4: Why I Quit Zombie School*. New York, NY: Scholastic, 2011.

Valentino, Serena. *How to Be a Zombie*. Somerville, MA: Candlewick Press, 2010.

Woog, Adam. *Zombies* (Monsters and Mythical Creatures). San Diego, CA: ReferencePoint Press, 2011.

WEBSITES

Because of the changing nature of Internet links, Rosen Publishing has developed an online list of websites related to the subject of this book. This site is updated regularly. Please use this link to access this list:

http://www.rosenlinks.com/UTP/Zomb

INDEX

A

Africa, 10, 11, 16, 17, 20, 42

B

Benin, 11, 17, 20
bodies, 4, 6, 8, 12, 17, 32
bokor, 11–12, 28, 29–31, 32
books, 6, 10, 13, 14, 16, 20–21,
    33–34, 36, 41
brains, 4, 8, 15

C

Caribbean, 10, 16, 20

F

Felix-Mentor, Felicia, 24,
    27–28, 30
films, 4, 6, 8, 10, 15–16, 21–22,
    23, 35, 41
folklore, Haitian, 4, 6, 8,
    11–12, 15, 17, 38

G

games, 6, 7, 8, 13, 14, 41–42
grave, 4, 6, 12, 15, 20, 21

H

Haiti, 4, 10–11, 17, 20, 21, 24,
    28, 30, 31, 32, 42
horror fiction, 4, 35–36

L

legends, zombie, 6, 13–14,
    16, 17

M

movies, 6, 7, 8, 13, 14, 15, 21,
    22–23, 25, 33–35

N

Narcisse, Clairvius, 28–30,
    31–32
Night of the Living Dead, 22,
    23, 33